I feel frightened

HODDER
Wayland

an imprint of Hodder Children's Books

When I'm frightened I feel like...

a quivering jelly
on a plate,

a shivering mouse
that's just met
a cat,

or Little Miss Muffet
face to face with
her spider.

When I'm frightened...

I put my hands over my eyes,

I dive under the bedcovers,

I hide behind
my dad.

7

All sorts of things frighten
me. I feel frightened
when I go upstairs
on my own...

I'm frightened when I think there are spiders under my bed.

But any spider I find is much more
frightened of me!

I like to play hide and seek!

And even though I'm frightened when dad makes me jump, I still want to play it again!

I felt really frightened on my first day at school...

but I had such a good time that I
didn't want to go home!

The first time I slept at Grandma's house I felt frightened.

But Grandma came
and sat by my bed.
She told me stories
until I fell asleep.

My big brother said the dentist was awful and I wouldn't like going at all.

But the dentist didn't worry me.
She said I had lovely teeth!

20

Sometimes I'm frightened when I watch scary programmes on television. But I know it's only make-believe!

When I start to feel frightened...

it helps if I sing or whistle.

It helps if I tell myself not to be so silly,

or if I pretend I'm a fearless superhero!

It helps if I talk to
my teddy,

24

or remind myself that everyone feels frightened sometimes, even grown-ups.

My dad hates riding on a roller coaster.
He says he feels really scared.

Mum says she's frightened of flying.
She'd rather keep her feet on the ground.

But sometimes when you feel
frightened...

you just have to
be brave!

What do you do when
you feel frightened?

Notes for parents and teachers

Read the book with children either individually or in groups. Ask them how they feel when they are frightened. Which of the ideas on pages 4-5 is closest to how they feel, or do they picture their fear in different ways? Ask them to illustrate how they feel.

Help children to compose short poems that tell us about their fears:
    When shadows lurk in the bedroom,
    When a storm is raging at night,
    When fireworks make loud noises,
        These are my fears.

Alternatively they might begin each line with, 'I am frightened...'
    I am frightened of what might be under my bed.
    I am frightened of dogs when they growl at me,
    I am frightened...

Children could also write about the things that frighten other members of the family.

Can children think of situations where they expected to be frightened, but then found out that there was really nothing to worry about? Look at the pages that feature going to school for the first time and visiting the dentist. Could they write about an experience such as these in a way that might reassure others?

Can children think of words that we use to say how frightened we are? These might include dread, panic, tremble, shake, shiver, quake, scared, horrified. What do children understand by such phrases as; 'scare the living daylights out of', 'put the wind up', 'make your knees 'knock', 'frighten out of your wits'? Can they think of other phrases that we use? Children may enjoy illustrating such phrases in an amusing way.

Some children might like to act out situations that frighten them. Other children can offer ways in which these fears might be lessened.

Through the sharing of picture books, such as those mentioned on page 32, talk to children about their fears and help them to come to terms with them.

The above ideas will help to satisfy a number of attainment targets in the National Curriculum Guidelines for English at Key Stage 1.

Books to read

The Ankle Grabber, *Jumble Joan*, *The Flat Man* and *Scare Yourself to Sleep*, (The 'Creepies' series), written by Rose Impey and illustrated by Moira Kemp, (Ragged Bears, 1989). In each book, particular fears are explored and resolved.

Can't You Sleep Little Bear? written by Martin Waddell and illustrated by Barbara Firth, (Walker Books, 1988). This award winning book should help to dispel fear of the dark.

This is the Bear and the Scary Night written by Sarah Hayes and illustrated by Helen Craig, (Walker Books, 1991). A lost bear is found again after a scary night in the park.

Two Terrible Frights written by Jim Aylesworth and illustrated by Eileen Christelow, (Picture Puffin, 1990). A little girl and a mouse meet up in the middle of the night while looking for bedtime snacks.

Starting School by Janet and Allan Ahlberg, (Picture Puffin, 1990). A reassuring read for children who are apprehensive about taking this big step.